MAKE IT YOUR SEASON

By
Vance C. Stanton
© 2012

Copyright © 2012, Vance C. Stanton

Make It Your Season
By: Vance C. Stanton

ISBN-10:
ISBN-13:

All rights reserved solely by the author. Except where designated, the author certifies that all contents are original and do not infringe upon the legal rights of any other person or work. No part of this book may be reproduced in any form without the permission of the publisher.

Printed in the United States
10 9 8 7 6 5 4 3 2 1

Cover concept by: Vance C. Stanton

Presented To:

To contact the author go to:
www.MakeItYourSeason.com

Contents

Acknowledgments

Preface

Chapter 1   Finding Out What You Want in Life: Big 10%

Chapter 2   A Step in the Right Direction: Major 20%

Chapter 3   Getting into the World of What You Want: Cool 30%

Chapter 4   The Importance of Having a Mentor: Most Valuable 40%

Chapter 5   Start Seeing Results: Halfway 50%

Chapter 6   Don't Quit. You've Just Started: Keep Going 60%

Chapter 7   Getting Tired Is Part of the Process: Perseverance 70%

Chapter 8   The Fruit of Your Labor: Happy 80%

Chapter 9   It's Your Season: Won the Lottery 90%

Chapter 10 Managing Your Season: Watchful 100%

Acknowledgments

I would like to thank God for blessing me and giving me the spirit of perseverance to succeed in what can be a cruel world. I would like to thank all my clients at the barbershop who gave me words of wisdom to help me in my pursuits of becoming a better person and in becoming an accomplished author. I would like to thank my Pastor John L. Andrews, for being the dad I never had. I would like to thank all the men and women that are working hard every day for what they believe in.

Last but not least, I would like to thank the people who once doubted me on achieving success—I used that energy as motivation to reach my goal.

–Vance C. Stanton

Preface

One of the most important questions that anyone could ask is what's life all about? After spending time pondering this great question, I came up with these answers. Life is about living with a purpose and making your visions and dreams become a reality. Life is about being happy and becoming the person that you aspire to be. Life is about doing the things that you enjoy doing most, but without boundaries or limitations.

That's the life for me, and that's the life I live now—the life that I once only dreamed about.

You see, it was important that I took a close look at my life and asked the tough questions: Who am I and what am I to be? I found that those questions were at the core of all of my desires and what I wanted out of life. Without knowing who you are, and what it is you want to be, all of life's pursuits can lead to dead ends.

This is where so many people get trapped and become disillusioned with themselves.

When we are born into this world, none of us come with instructions. Life seems to be one big mystery, as we meet challenge after challenge. Without the proper guidance and support, we are practically doomed to fail, because the world is not so accommodating to those who don't know where they fit in. This is why it is so important to have the proper interest, influences, and pursuits in your life. My life was aimless until I discovered my system for success that works.

Today, I love the way that my life is set up. I'm happy with myself, my affairs are in order, and I'm prosperous. I have freedom to do the things that I want to do, and I enjoy life.

With all the unnecessary distractions in life out of the way (e.g., drowning in debt), I can focus on my passion in life—

helping others to become better with their lives.

There is a song by Lady Gaga titled "You Were Born This Way." The gist of the song says that "it doesn't matter where you were born, your life is perfect the way it is." When I apply that song to my life, I can say that even though I was born in Chicago's projects, my life was perfect the way it was, because I was born that way. And the socioeconomic status that I was born into didn't matter because from that very point I could change and better my life—and that's what I did. Words of wisdom say, "Never let bad circumstances or surroundings define who you are." You were born you, and you were also born to change. But in order to change, you have to take responsibility for your life by accepting where you are in your life. That's what I did, and that's how I made it my season—by taking responsibility.

Being raised in the Ida B. Wells housing projects, there wasn't a lot to look forward to. I had no father at home, and my mother WAS a substance abuser. Under those unfavorable circumstances, I lacked motivation and had no hope for a brighter future. I couldn't see myself becoming successful. However, years later, God blessed me, and I was able to turn everything around when I began to "sow and plant" (work hard) for the life I wanted, until I reached my "dream life."

Everyone has a dream life, but when life seems unfair, the dream you have may be the only glimpse you have at the time of a better life. I didn't settle for the life people thought I should have, and neither should you. Your life is worth you getting all that you desire from it. "YOUR LIFE IS TRULY WORTH YOUR HAPPINESS." Napoleon Hill, author of "Think and Grow Rich," once said, "What the mind of a man can conceive and believe it can achieve." What that means is, when you have an idea of what you want and you believe you can achieve it, you will find the recipe for success.

My passion is helping people make it their season and I'm living proof that you can make it your season. There's only one difference between those who make it their season and those who do not: those who reach their dream life status take all the necessary steps in order to achieve it. However, for those who are unsure of what a step in the right direction is, let this book act as a compass to point you in the right direction and provide you with a plan to succeed in every area of your life.

Even though I have reached my dream life, I try hard to avoid the pitfall of thinking that I know everything—no one does. However, there is one thing I'm certain of, "we can change" and become whatever we want to be in life. To me, life is like a big block of ice: cold and square. Though others may see that block of ice as valueless, you are the artist who sees the beauty and value in that cold block of ice, and it's your JOB to bring the beautiful image within that ice out for all to see.

You can make the huge block of ice into what you want it to be. You are the artist, and depending on how well you sculpt your life, you will reveal how skilled of an artist you are, as with the block of ice. Your life should be a masterpiece, comprised of ALL you want out of it. The only difference between you and Picasso is that he designed masterpieces of art on canvas and you are making a masterpiece of your life and your future.

No matter what your circumstances are in life, if you are willing to take the necessary steps, you can create a life you love and enjoy. It does not make a difference whether you have physical limitations or whether you have suffered from things like abuse or neglect; you have the power to forgive your past, own your future and "make it your season."

"Having an appreciative attitude toward life is the main ingredient for a good life, because it could always be worse."

The best part of life shouldn't be our past but the present moment, the "Now." Since our time on earth is so short, making the most of the time we do have is all part of "making it our season" and "owning the moment."

Preface

Making it your season is about how well your life flows and how much enjoyment you can get out of your life. You shouldn't let society dictate to you what you can have out of life. Life should be personal, and you are to customize your life. Like a tailor who sews and cuts a garment until it fits just right, make sure you tailor your life so it's a perfect fit as well.

I can truly say that the life that I have now is no accident. I "planted my life" for the prosperity that I have now. What do I mean when I say planted? "Planting" is putting in all the work necessary to succeed and waiting patiently for results (harvest). I've been working on my journey of life for years, and now the harvest is here. I am having a great time living the life I prepared for myself, and by the end of this book you will be on the road to your dream life. I present to you "Make It Your Season."

Chapter 1

Finding Out What You Want In Life

THE BIG 10%

Do you know what area of your life needs to be improved? If you took time to identify some of the issues you struggle with in everyday life, you could answer this question, rather quickly. Wouldn't it be nice if you had a magical wand that you could wave and make your problems disappear? Or, what about simply wishing your problems away? Wouldn't it be nice if you had three wishes to change anything in your life? What would those three wishes be?

I became curious and wanted to know what were the top things people wanted most out of life. To answer that question I went to Google's search engine and did a search, for the top three things people want out of life. The Google results came back in this order: (1) more happiness and less stress, (2) more money, (3) to be loved for who they are.

Now that we know what the Google search results said about the top three things people want most out of life, the question is, "What do you wish for?" Do you wish for better health/weight loss, more organization, getting out of major debt, becoming a better parent to your child/children, or to be more in tune with your spiritual side? No matter what your wish is in life, this book will show you how to get all that you wish for in life, to the point where every day will feel like you won the mega millions lottery. ☺

Before we go any further, there are a few things that you need to know. In this book I utilize a simple system that will help you to measure how successful you are in pursuing each one of your goals.

With each chapter title, there is a subtitle and a percentage value. Chapter one starts out with 10%, all the way to the tenth chapter, where the goal is 100%. Each chapter (or 10%) has an important theme that when applied to your life, progressively you become better until you reach 100% in every part of your life: your dream life. Sounds good? Then if so, with a little determination and focus, before you know it you'll be at 100%.

I use this system, and the reason I know it works is because I have already reached the 100% mark in my own life, and I'm going to show you how to reach 100% in all areas of your life. *Make It Your Season* is a winning formula for success.

Another reference point is that, after you finish reading this book I recommend that you keep it close by so you can return to it at any time for guidance during your quest to accomplish your "dreams".

At this point, it is important that I define two concepts so you won't get lost in some of the terminology I use throughout this book. The first concept in this book is titled "Make It Your Season." When it comes to "making it your season," it means you are at the point where you have achieved wholeness in every area of your life personally and professionally. In other words, that means taking the time to go through all areas of your life, eliminating the things you don't want in your life until your life is full of good things. You therefore get the ultimate enjoyment out of life and become secure and confident with yourself because nothing's lacking.

In order to "make it your season," you need to choose areas of your life that you target for improvement. These areas that you choose to improve are called *seasonal choices*. A *seasonal choice* is a specific area of your life that is lacking something that you work on improving, making it a part of your life that you love. For example, making more money or losing weight are two examples of seasonal choices that a person can choose to improve in their life.

What's Your Big Thing?

The late, great Dr. Stephen Covey, businessman and motivational speaker, in one of his inspirational seminars, used a bucket of rocks to make a very important point about using a system of process of elimination. In his illustration, he took a bucket of rocks filled to the rim and poured them out onto a table. After doing that, he called a young lady from out of the audience to come up and place all the rocks back in the bucket. To everyone's surprise, she wasn't able to get all the rocks back in the bucket.

That's when Dr. Covey stepped in and said, "Place the big rocks in the bucket first and then put the smaller rocks in after the big rocks." (The bigger rocks represented important things, and the small rocks represented small, not-so-important things.) After following his instructions of putting all the big rocks in first (remember the big rocks represent big priority), the woman was able to get all the rocks back into the bucket. Here's what we all can learn from this simple illustration: deal with the big issues first in our life, then all the little issues. It is important to prioritize and take care of the big things first in life.

Being inspired by Dr. Covey, I began to evaluate my own life and chose six areas of my life that needed to be improved.

However, since we are all individuals who have different needs, it's totally up to you what your seasonal choices will be.

My first seasonal choice was in the area of spirituality, which I'm not going to expound on in detail. However, I will say that I felt it necessary to develop a relationship with God first. Because even if I had obtained everything that life has to offer, without God in my life, everything isn't much at all.

My second seasonal choice was to achieve *financial freedom*, which I expound on in detail throughout this book. I would like to define financial freedom this way: *where you are no longer being stressed out over money and debt.* Your expenditures are under control, you maintain a budget and do not live beyond your means, but you have time and the financial means to enjoy life the way you want.

When it came to my finances, I had to undergo a complete makeover. My finances were a mess. I could turn my pants pockets inside out and not a dime would fall out. With the pockets of my trousers turned inside out, it looked like I had bunny ears.

I had the finances of a college kid who has no job. With school being the job, it's possible to go days with not enough to eat, because you don't get a paycheck from a chemistry class.

Why I Chose Finances

I needed income so I could afford the lifestyle I wanted. Let's face it; whether we claim to be materialistic or not, just about everything we do in life is centered around us maintaining a level of comfort. For example, most of us want to get our children in the best schools possible, right? The reason is, we want our children to have the best education so more career opportunities will be available to them. The better the career, the more income; the more income, the better chances at living a more prosperous life.

Having the right income level allows us to obtain and maintain a desired level of comfort. The things that make us comfortable tend to affect every decision we make, from the place we live, to the type of car we drive, to the shoes and clothes we wear, to the food we eat, to the way we style our hair. Most life decisions we make are all about what works best for us. Therefore, I knew that if I improved the financial part of my life, I would be more balanced and financially able to do the other things that I wanted to do, like traveling, taking trips to tropical places like Hawaii, shopping at high-end stores, and philanthropy (giving back to the less fortunate). Therefore, I stopped accepting my current situation and set out to make a change to make more money.

Be Clear On Choice

Now that you know what two of my seasonal choices are, I'm going to expound on the question "What's your seasonal choice?" Could your choice possibly be weight loss so you can feel more comfortable in your skin? Or perhaps, your choice is organization so you can have more order and less clutter? What about learning a new language so you can be bilingual?

The only caution to this whole formula to a successful life is to actually choose one thing to work on. You can't be double mined about what you want out of life. You have to be certain about your seasonal choice, or else the system will be limited in working for you. A lot of people don't get the most out of life because they waver in what it is they really want. Knowing exactly what it is you want out of life is called *clarity of purpose*. You must have clarity about your life. For example if you need good health, you need to clear yourself from toxic habits and relationships. You can't say "I need good health" and keep doing unhealthy things at the same time. If you do that, you become what is known as being "double-minded." You have to choose what you need most and start to work on that first. Clarity of purpose is the most powerful statement ever because it is the gateway to all success. When you have clarity, you know exactly what you want, unlike the double-minded person being unstable in all their ways.

The choice is your's—your seasonal choices can be anything you want them to be, because this system is sure to lead you to victory. As Dr. Covey suggested, you should prioritize your seasonal choices and deal with the biggest concerns first. Knowing exactly what you want is The Big 10%.

Chapter 2

A Step In The Right Direction

THE MAJOR 20%

Making a decision to do something is never enough by itself. If you get stuck in the imaginary but never take action, nothing will ever change, except for the fact that you have wasted time. This is where many people struggle, never getting off the ground. Is this you, a person who'd rather procrastinate than take action? A way to see how easy it is to procrastinate can be seen in the answer of the riddle below.

> There were three monkeys sitting on a bridge, one monkey in the middle and one on each side. The monkey in the middle decided to jump. How many monkeys were left?

If you are like most people, your answer would probably be two. But the correct answer is three. Why? Because the monkey in the middle didn't actually jump, he only *decided* to.

Every day in life we say that we're going to do things that we wind up not doing. So we must be careful that we're not just saying we're going to do things.

In order for any idea to take on the full meaning of the word "decision," action must be present and applied.

Don't Let Excuses Hold You Back

At the end of the day, all life's pursuits boils down to if you are taking steps to reach your dream or not. Oftentimes, it can seem like we have a good excuse as to why we can't make progress toward our longing dreams. But the truth of the matter is that we are the only ones who can stop us from taking steps toward what we truly want. The power to succeed from within has to be greater than ALL else around you or you will not succeed.

I could have used the so-called "good excuse" that the neighborhood I grew up in was the reason I couldn't become successful. Or I could have let the fact that I never knew my father detour me. But I didn't. I didn't let anything or any excuse stop me from my dreams, so neither should you. I've heard people say they have too many children to go back to school and get the degree they always wanted. I've heard people say their spouse doesn't support their dreams, so they settle for a life that has become mundane, plain, and unfulfilling.

I caution you not to be a victim of helping everyone but yourself. People will care about your dreams and goals only as much as you make them care. Also, in order to make people care, it has to be a priority to you before it can become a priority for someone else. Don't be a pushover, allowing everyone in your life to be happy except you. Stand up for what you want, and believe in you!

The Courageous Step

"If you start taking small steps toward your dream, pretty soon your dream will become a reality."

Allow me to tell you that accomplishing your dreams is not going to come without a fight. Have you ever heard the saying "anything that's worth having is worth fighting for"? That saying is true. But in terms of *you* being happy in life, the victory will definitely be worth the fight.

One of my clients from barbering is a firefighter. After coming from a big fire, his lieutenant would always say, "Those flames were strong today, but I'm glad we all made it out alive." Then he would say, "But we knew the job was dangerous when we took it." Just as it is tough with being a firefighter, you're going to have to fight to make it your season. Know that when you're going after making it your season, people/things aren't going to concede to you easily all the time. If I could be the lieutenant at the fire station right now, I would say, making your dream life a reality is a tough job but you definitely can do it.

Scouting For Steps

My second seasonal choice was to improve my finances, but to make that happen I had to put that choice into action. I wanted to make more money, so I was looking for ways to do so.

"Opportunities are always present. You just have to know them when you see them or hear them."

When you clearly know what the need is in your life, you are apt to act when opportunities present themselves. Your senses become more keen because you're hungry, looking for ways to satisfy the craving. Your mind goes into overdrive to seek out the right connections to achieve your objectives.

Finding Choices

With a spirit of expectation and an open mind, I was on a mission to succeed, and soon I struck gold. I wanted to make more money, so I was looking for ways to do so.

While attending my aunt's fortieth birthday party, I saw a gentleman there taking photographs of those in attendance. I noticed that he had a professional camera, and I watched him working the crowd methodically, going to each table taking people's pictures. He just walked right up to everyone seated at the table and asked them to smile for the camera, and without hesitation people readily obliged. He also had some props set up for those who desired to take photographs with a more scenic background. He also had his printer and lighting equipment all set up.

After taking their snapshot, he would let them know that if they were interested in getting those memorable photos, they could get them for a cost of ten or twenty dollars. Something else I noticed was that just about everyone there got their picture taken on the backdrop. Needless to say, that photographer cleaned up at that party, making hundreds of dollars, not to mention the fact that each photo he took was a referral for future events.

As I watched him work, there were two intriguing things about this photographer that caught my attention right away. First of all, the work he was doing didn't seem to be too difficult. He wasn't breaking his back with physical labor. Secondly, he was getting paid right there on the spot. After seeing this, I put myself in that scenario and I *saw* myself being successful doing the same thing. Instantly I was captivated by the possibilities, and I made a decision that changed my life. The decision was that being an independent photographer was how I was going to reach financial independence. I had made a decision, and now came the plan to put my decision into action.

VISUALIZE YOURSELF BEING SUCCESSFUL

Sometimes we let great ideas pass us by because we're slow pushing the ACTION button. We look for the perfect time to act, and the truth is, there's no such thing as the perfect time. You just have to know what you want and then act on the opportunity when it's presented—visualizing yourself being successful.

I wasn't trying to be a "rocket scientist." I was just trying to make some extra money and it wasn't necessary to reinvent the wheel to do so at this party. So I seized the opportunity and went over and talked to the photographer to see what was up with the business. However, to my surprise he was not engaging. He was about his business and didn't want to hear anything besides taking photos and making money.

Important point: Don't be easily deterred from your goals, because at some point you are sure to bump into some opposition. A person who could be useful to you at first may put you off or be uninterested in helping because they don't know you or feel obligated to help you.

The Power Of Quick Thinking

A door you thought was opened to you could be closed in your face. Therefore, you must be prepared to overcome rejection with persistence.

Quickly, I realized that this person may have rejected my offer to show me the ropes as a waste of his time. Time is money, right? So that's when I came up with another plan that worked. I stepped it up and made him an offer to pay him $75 for an hour of his time to teach me a little about the photography business (I wanted him to give me some insider information). Ever heard the phrase "money talks"? That saying is true. Offering him that $75 for an hour of his time spoke directly to that *wasting my time* issue, and that same evening at my aunt's party, we scheduled a meeting for two days later.

As it turned out, that was my first step in becoming financially independent and having a successful career as a professional photographer. Since then, I have gone on to make thousands of dollars in a day, and my skills have taken me before some great people. I have taken photos of several prominent people, including famous people like Barack Obama, Chicago

Mayor Rahm Emanuel, Beyoncé and Jay Z, Steve Harvey and other famous entertainers and comedians. All of this started when I took the first step toward wanting to increase my income.

Your First Move

No matter what your seasonal choice is, you will need to take that crucial first step in making it your season. If your goal is to lose weight, you could perhaps join the local gym, buy a scale to monitor your weight, or find a diet that works for you.

It doesn't matter what your seasonal choice is—you just have to find the right tools and make them work for you. Take a step and challenge yourself. That's called The Major 20%.

Chapter 3

Getting Into The World of What You Want

COOL 30%

Have you ever heard the saying "you are known by the company that you keep"? I have found this is very true. One might ask, what does whom I associate with have to do with what direction in life I am heading? After all, that's them, this is me—right? Well, yes, it is true you are different from your associates, but that is not the only thing to consider. The *law of association* informs us that people tend to associate with people like themselves. You are attracted to individuals like you or you become like the people with whom you associate. Both ways, the effect can be dramatic depending upon the circumstances or the nature of your relationships.

Hang Around Positive People

No matter what the common bond, people associate with people like themselves. Those who love basketball tend to associate with people who also play and watch basketball. On the flip side of that coin, a serious baller probably wouldn't be very interested in a golf tournament, unless golf is another one of his interests. A person may have several things they can do, but it's only the things that interest them that will become the basis for association with other people. This *law of association* applies to both virtues and vices (good things and bad things).

In order to become successful in any endeavor, it is important that you be in the right environment and surround yourself with the right people who can and/or will help you become what you wish to be.

Hang Around Your Seasonal Choice

This is what I did: I started hanging out with photographers. I surrounded myself with photographer after photographer.

I started asking questions about the pros and cons of the business. I started educating myself on the terminology and tricks of the trade to improve my skill set. I became like a sponge soaking up all the knowledge I could on how to be successful in photography.

The photographers who trained me told me interesting things like where to purchase the supplies I needed and where to get the best deals on miscellaneous items. I learned what types of camera lenses to purchase, what types of props to have, and what type of camera bag to carry. Then there was the financial end of the business, learning how much I should be charging for photos and what percentage I should be paying a party or wedding planner if they referred me for a job. I learned which cameras took the best photos in different light settings and what were the best photo-printers to have. To keep from being ripped off, they even showed me how to detect counterfeit money instantly.

Likewise, you have to immerse yourself in the world of the goal you choose and learn all you can about your field. For example, if your seasonal choice is *organization*, you need to immerse yourself in any and everything that has to do with being organized. You should be doing things like reading books and magazines on organization and watching programs or instructional videos on organization. Then you would also need to be interactive, and get out and talk to people who have mastered organization. From them you can learn effective techniques of organization. Anything on organization should interest you because this is the world you are getting into, the world of organization. That's called The Cool 30%.

Chapter 4

The Importance of Having a Mentor

THE MOST VALUABLE 40%

If there is one thing to which I can attribute my success in photography, I can say without hesitation that it was because I had a great mentor. The dictionary defines the word mentor as: *a trusted counselor or guide, a tutor, or a coach.* From this definition, we can see that a good mentor can have a dramatic effect on our development to success. It is important that your mentor is someone you can be comfortable with.

The Professional Mentoree

Prior to becoming involved with photography, it became clear to me that whenever I excelled at something, each time there was someone there to mentor me in my pursuits. I already had a lot of experience trying to do things on my own and failing.

It's truly much easier to have someone who has gone before you who has already made the rookie mistakes to show you how to do things properly. Whether you're in a classroom setting or everyday life, you need a mentor to show you the protocol of life's pursuits.

"Once I realized the benefits of being mentored with photography, I began to think about how I used the concept of being mentored in different areas of my life."

One of my first areas of being mentored was in my pursuit to become a licensed barber. I remember I used to go to this particular barbershop just to watch this ultra-talented barber cut hair. By doing so, I had a role model as to what it was like to be a successful barber. I was able to observe techniques on styling. I was able to observe how he interacted with his clients. I was able to observe what type of clippers, liners, and stylers he was using to do the different styles of haircuts. Then I took the next step by building a rapport with him. By developing a rapport with him, I was able to interact and ask him questions about cutting techniques and the profession in general. It wasn't long after that, that I finished barber college and perfected what my mentor had taught me while I was carefully observing him. It didn't happen all it once—it was a step-by-step process.

Another example of improvement through being mentored occurred while I attended church. I quickly saw the value of associating with the brothers who knew the Bible very well and knew how to live according to its principles. The result is I'm further along in my faith and much more knowledgeable about the Bible. Still another example of self-improvement is when I wanted to learn about a healthy diet. I found a mentor to help me understand the benefits of better nutrition, and set out to maintain a healthy lifestyle.

Mentor Appreciation

The point I'm making from all these examples is that I learned to appreciate the benefits of having a mentor. It is so vital to have someone show you the way to do things as opposed to learning only by trial and error. Therefore, once you get a mentor, you are pointed in the right direction and are well on your way to achieving success in your seasonal choice.

In everything that I have discussed so far, whether it was being mentored by the professional photographers, watching the barber at the barbershop, my associations at church, or better nutritional habits, I began to see similar aspects of how to improve in every area. It didn't matter that none of these areas had anything in common, the principles for improvement were the same. That's when I began to see that there is a system to becoming successful—a practical system of success that works in any area of life. I came to the conclusion that I would put this system to work, first in my life, and then share with others how to become successful using my proven system.

There may be people who do not understand the importance of having a good mentor, but that can be easily changed. The fact that I realized that I needed a mentor meant that I had become teachable, and that I was ready to learn. I didn't think I knew it all already. Being a know-it-all can be an issue where many people fall short, thinking no one can teach them.

Unfortunately, some people will not let you help them. They have to do everything the hard way. They won't humble themselves and swallow their pride to ask for the necessary guidance to make it. Their mind-set is often "me, myself and I," the same mentality that will keep you unsuccessful and ultimately unfulfilled.

Picking the right mentor is just as important as choosing the right seasonal choice. Your mentor should be someone you can respect and honor for the gifts they possess. The first question you should ask yourself about a potential mentor is, are they themselves accomplished and successful in the field of interest that you're inquiring about? In other words, taking your cues on starting a business from someone who has never owned a business is a recipe for failure, so be careful when choosing your guide.

Mentor Found

I had learned a lot from the previous photographers I had met but now I was looking for a new challenge. The challenge was finding a photographer I could imitate who had his/her own site/lounge where they were making big money every weekend.

I started out asking everyone I knew what was the number one place in Chicago where there was a photographer making a lot of money like the first guy I had met at my aunt's fortieth birthday party.

At this point, I learned something interesting about people in my pursuit of making it my season. I learned that all the answers we need in life can be found in other people's experiences—another good reason for surrounding yourself with virtuous people.

When you get ready to meet your mentor, start asking around for the top person in your field of interest. Shortly after you start asking, you will be on your way to meet your mentor. ☺

"People will point you in the right direction if you're asking the right people the right questions."

Once I began inquiring about where I could go meet up with a very successful photographer, on several occasions I was told about a place called the Couture City Lounge. A lot of people said there was an older gentleman there with long grey hair who always had a line of people waiting to have their photos taken.

So I went to that lounge and found out it was true. Just as I had been told, there was a photographer who had a long line of people waiting to have their photos taken. That was the first time I had ever seen a photographer that successful. And to my surprise, this was the same place where celebrities came to perform and have after parties. I could clearly see that he was making money hand over fist. And that's when I saw myself making money like that and being a celebrity photographer, too. Having the same level of success then became my goal. But the only way to become just like him was for him to become my mentor.

"Remember, if your seasonal pick is making more sales on a commission-based job, observe the account executive that sells the most units and adopt their techniques."

Compliment Your Mentor

When you meet your mentor, have a sincere dialogue with them and ask if you could observe them in action. Acknowledge their accomplishments and success. It's "much easier" to get help from someone to whom you have been kind. Most of the time people don't mind you watching as long as you are considerate and do not become annoying or get in their way.

Compliment your mentor when you first see them. Compliment them when you leave and let them know that they are doing a great job. Complimenting your mentor on their skills is a quick way to gain favor with them.

Be Persistent With Your Mentor

Always be persistent. I went to Couture City Lounge for weeks on end, just getting familiar with the photographer and letting him get familiar with me. Once Chris saw that I was serious and not going to waste his time, he became even more enthusiastic about helping me because it was obvious that I wanted to be successful. You have to be persistent with your mentor and be serious about your seasonal choice.

Stay Focused

Whenever you have set your goals to succeed, you must always beware of distractions that can knock you off your game. I was not going to the Couture City Lounge to have fun. I was going to see my mentor, not to pick up the ladies, not to dance and party with the big shots, but to learn how to be better at my trade. While everyone else was there spending money having a good time, I was watching my mentor. I watched his techniques closely, and I implemented the same strategies he used in my own business.

Soon, not only was I watching him work, but I was also helping him handle his clientele. I was giving him a hand putting the photos he took in the photo sleeves, and I helped him collect the money he was making. This is very important: You must have someone's confidence in order for them to let you handle their cash. Loyalty and trustworthiness are necessary characteristics of a successful mentoree. After several sessions with learning from a professional, I now had business cards, the equipment I needed, and most of all, the knowledge I needed to start making money of my own.

Making Your Mentor Proud

You should volunteer your time to your mentor in exchange for knowledge. The main thing you are supposed to do when you come in contact with your mentor is grow into being like them. Please don't become a burden to your mentor by not growing. You should be investing in becoming more like your mentor, and that's going to take both time and money.

When you show up to meet your mentor, show him or her your growth. Let them know that you're listening to them by following up on the things they tell you to do and buying the things they tell you to purchase. Those few tips will definitely make your mentor proud of you, and your mentor will keep giving you pointers so that you can keep growing.

Getting The Overflow

Since I kept going to the lounge where my mentor had a thriving business, the more his business grew, the more he needed my help. Even though I was his student, he knew that he had trained me well enough to handle his overflow (the work he couldn't get around to). So he started giving me jobs that he couldn't do because he was so busy. The fact that I represented his interests so well was a plus, and he rewarded me by giving me some of his business. My hard work, and his confidence in me ended up taking my business to the next level.

Likewise, you are to represent the interests of your mentor so well that they will offer you all they have to give, and with that kind of rapport, you can take your seasonal choice to the next level. Getting a Mentor is The Most Valuable 40%.

Chapter 5

Start Seeing Results

HALFWAY 50%

After you have made a decision on what you want out of life, have taken steps in that direction, have immersed yourself in your field of interest, and have had the guidance of a mentor, you should be seeing results. However, it is very important to understand that timing is everything, and time goes by so fast when you're busy achieving your seasonal choice. So don't get caught up in timing. "Don't focus on time, focus on your seasonal choice." You are halfway to reaching your goal.

Estimated Time For A Seasonal Choice

"The most time that it should take to complete any seasonal choice is twelve years, and that seasonal choice would be becoming a doctor." With this system, it should not take you more than twelve years to have your dream life. Some seasonal choices can be achieved in as little as three months when you're dealing with choices like organization. Some may take two years when you're dealing with something like paying off debt.

Nevertheless, when it comes to time frame, your first seasonal choice should be the one that will take the longest time to complete because it should be the biggest obstacle you'll have to overcome. Your second, third, and fourth choices should take less time to complete. That's if you use Dr. Covey's system of putting the big things first.

How Time Flies

Let me give you two examples of how time flies. My first example is for people in the age range of thirty-five years old. If you are thirty-five, that means you have been out of high school almost twenty years. Most people would probably say that twenty years is a long time. However, when you look back at being out of high school, twenty years probably doesn't seem like that long of a time. The second example is watching your kids grow up. I remember when my son was born four years ago. When I look at him now, and think back four years, it seems like just yesterday he was born. The point I'm making is that we all have experiences where time flies if you think about it. Since time goes by so fast, that's more reason to knock out the bigger seasonal challenges first.

"You're going to want to be ready, because before you know it, you'll be in your season."

Half Full

At this point in my seasonal choice I had invested in a camera, a backdrop, some printers, business cards, and everything else I needed to be a successful photographer. I invested heavily in my seasonal choice, and you will also have to diligently invest in yours.

"Whatever you put into your choice is what you're going to get out of it."

I was taking photos for a year and a half at this point in my seasonal choice. I was earning approximately $300 a night from various photography jobs in addition to the money I was making at the barbershop. I was starting to see results of my financial seasonal choice coming to life.

By this time you should be seeing some results because you have been following the system. If your goal is losing weight, you should already be losing some pounds. If your goal is learning a new language, you should already know a few words in that language. If your goal is getting a degree, you should already be enrolled in college classes at this point. And if your goal is learning how to cook, you should have already cooked something simple like brown rice by this point. At this point in making it your season, the reason why you would be halfway to your goals is, you should be gravitating incrementally toward your seasonal choice. Taking it step-by-step and listening to your mentor's advice.

In the next few chapters, I'm going to show you how I went from making hundreds of dollars a day to thousands of dollars a day. I'll show you how you can go from losing ten pounds to having a dream body, how you can go from learning a few sentences of a new language to speaking that language fluently. I will show you how to go from passing that first midterm to earning that degree, and from preparing that first gourmet meal to becoming a master chef. Anything is possible when you have the elements of success in place. You're at Halfway 50%.

Chapter 6

Don't Quit. You've Just Started

KEEP GOING 60%

One of the main problems people have with just about any self-improvement system is being consistent with the plan. A lot of people give up at this point because they are not happy with small gains. Unfortunately, we live in a society where people want instant gratification with everything. However, it is important that we do not overlook the value of small beginnings.

For example, a person whose goal is to have a dream body may not be satisfied with losing only a few pounds initially. With them having lost only a few pounds, their ideal weight is still a ways off. With only a small amount of weight loss at that point, they can easily become discouraged and want to quit.

Maybe a person wants to quit because after several foreign language lessons they have learned only a few sentences and are not yet fluent in their new language. Or, maybe they have earned some money but have not made what they were hoping to earn. This is the critical point where many people throw in the towel because discouragement sets in. That's because they don't recognize the importance and benefits of small beginnings.

Count Everything

"The one thing that people often forget is understanding the importance of all the effort that they have put in to even get to a small level of accomplishment."

All their energy invested was getting them closer to their goal. A lot of people forget about the small things like the legwork that was put in going to the gym. They forget about when they signed up for a membership, and the time they spent talking to trainers and having conversations about their exercise routine. Becoming discouraged, they forget about the time they invested reading exercise material, learning from instructional DVDs, and watching video footage from the Internet.

All the time and energy that you put into making your seasonal choice come to fruition counts for something. Don't abandon it. These efforts are like seeds that a farmer plants in the springtime. Often those tiny little seeds seem to be doing nothing for months. However, nothing could be further from the truth. Even though they are out of sight, those seeds are germinating, growing, and pushing up plants that will soon break through the ground, and will yield a great harvest in their season.

Remember, just because you have a goal does not mean that things will come easily. I learned by being mentored and much practice how to be an effective photographer. If I counted all the time that it took for me to learn my trade, it would be more hours than I would like to count. The $300 that I had been making was a good start, but I knew it wasn't where I wanted to be in my earnings, and that meant that I had more work to do. More planning, more promoting, and more producing leads to more prosperity. None of this happens by itself. You can't just believe you are going to be successful: you have to believe it, have a plan for becoming successful, and then do it.

So count the energy that you put into losing those ten pounds, count the energy that you put into signing up for classes and getting a good grade after taking that midterm exam.

I counted the time and energy that it took me to drive around, go to stores, search the Internet, go to get business cards, all the energy that I had put into photography before I was even making $300 a day. That's why counting the energy is so important because most people don't think about counting the energy they exasperated making a seasonal choice a reality. They don't realize how much work or how far they have come in a short amount of time. If you measure your accomplishments inch by inch, before you know it you will have gone a mile towards your goal.

Stay Focused On The Goal

Have you ever seen a target ring? Targets usually consist of several outer rings that get smaller as you approach the bull's-eye in the middle. You can gauge how well you are shooting as long as you are at least hitting the target. That's how I gauged my success. For example, the extra $300 a night I was earning was not the earnings on the bull's-eye that I was aiming for but it still was $300.

For a while, I was hitting the same $300 ring on the target. That's when I was able to determine that I needed to work harder to get better. What about you? What's your bull's-eye and how close are you coming to it? If you are hitting the outer rings, don't despair; that's measurable progress, because you are on the target. Don't get discouraged too quickly and give up. You have to keep on improving your aim until you are hitting your bull's-eye.

Although I wasn't making the thousands of dollars a day like the other photographers were, I was making $300 a night. I knew that if I could make that amount of money, eventually I would make $1,000 a night, and even own my own studio. By faith I had come this far, and by faith I was going to keep going until I was making thousands a night.

Don't Compare—Learn From Your Mentor

Another sense of unintended discouragement can come from other professionals themselves—even your mentor. Why? Because they make what's difficult look so easy, and when you try it, your arrows aren't flying in the same direction or you are overshooting your target. Remember that your mentor has probably been doing what they do for many years and during that time have developed successful techniques and expertise. And maybe when they started out, they weren't doing as well as you are currently. That's why you should never compare yourself to your mentor: you should be learning from your mentor. Besides, they're supposed to be better than you, or else they wouldn't be your mentor. Remember that there is no such thing as "microwave success." So don't become discouraged with small accomplishments—it takes a while to become a Pro, and that's Keep Going 60%.

Chapter 7

Getting Tired is Part of the Process

PERSEVERANCE 70%

As the saying goes, the race is not given to the swift nor to the strong, but to them that endure to the end. Just as this saying implies, endurance is more important than speed or strength. Endurance is what keeps you going even when you want to give up. As we follow the course for making it your season, one thing is for sure: at some point you're going to get tired.

I remember when it would be days when I would make only fifty dollars. Some days I would go out and would make no money at all—only taking one photo. Some days were better than others, but then again, some days were just plain bad. But particularly on those bad days, I experienced getting tired. I experienced wanting to throw in the towel. I experienced thinking that maybe I'd made the wrong decision on the career path that I had chosen. I experienced the frustration of not making the progress that I thought I should be making. These are all the roadblocks and obstructions that you find along the way. So my encouragement to you is, no matter what you may encounter along the way, stay in the race and keep pushing towards your prize.

The problem with setbacks is that they can cause you to want to give up. For example, if you have been vigorously working out and you lose twenty pounds, but suddenly you turn around and put twelve pounds back on, you may get discouraged. Perhaps the cause of the weight gain can be attributed to emotional eating caused by circumstances like a loved one passing away, losing your job, or going through a divorce. Serious challenges like these can easily cause you to lose focus and cause a setback.

Getting Tired Is Part of the Process

You may have gotten off track and now you feel like what's the use at this point? Because of disappointing setbacks you get tired and want to give up, but you should know you're not the only one. We all experience setback fatigue. But remember, that nothing worth accomplishing is going to be easy.

I knew that considering all the energy and time I had put into photography, I didn't want to give up. And it would have been hard to walk away from it because I had so much invested. I had to talk about it with people that I knew had my best interests in mind. I had to admit when I was feeling discouraged about making only $300 a night, some nights $50, and even worse, some nights, no money at all. Therefore, I talked to people and told them about how I was feeling discouraged. And to my surprise, when I was looking for a shoulder to cry on, what I readily got was, "But you've been doing good so far, and all you have to do is stick with it."

What I was experiencing is called "paying your dues." Paying your dues are the times you spend working hard to get ahead, only making a little progress and going through seemingly unnecessary changes. But there comes a time when you stop paying dues and start doing well. You just have to believe in yourself and hang in there.

On your journey to success, you are going to run into situations where you need some support and guidance. This is the whole purpose of having a mentor. I remember going to Chris the photographer and saying I was making only $50 on some jobs and sometimes no money. He said that he also had days like that, where he made only $50 and sometimes made nothing at all. I took comfort in knowing he had been through the same thing because he was a giant in my eyes. He said he didn't always make $1,500 or $2,000 a night, like he was now. He encouraged me to keep on going, because making $300 on a good night was a good start, and if I stuck with it, someday I'd be making a lot more.

As a result of listening to my mentor who was making it, I received the encouragement to keep going—those kinds of talks helped me to get over the hump when I was tired. Likewise, the encouragement you receive from someone who has your best interest in mind will give you the necessary push to help you endure to the end.

Encouragement Is Fuel

At some time or another, we have all been victims of our own false notions of how we imagine certain outcomes to be. We paint this picture in our minds of how everything will just fall into place and be hunky-dory ever after. However, when we run into life's pitfalls, potholes, and detours, and reality sets in, we quickly realize that we need to make some adjustments. At this juncture we have arrived at a critical point; here is where some encouraging words can make all the difference between quitting and continuing on.

For example, after learning that things were not always sunny for my mentor, I now understood that it's a normal experience wanting to quit when things are not going well. His words of wisdom also helped me get over the hump, and once I did, I pursued doing photo jobs with new determination. Why? The encouragement that I received was like pulling into a gas station and getting a fill-up.

When you are driving in a car and running low on gas, going forward brings a lot of stress because you are fearful of running out of gas and being stranded along the way. However, you have a whole new mind-set when you have a full tank of gas, because now you know you can go the distance. When I received the encouragement from my mentor, it was just like filling up my tank, and that carried me over to the point where I started making more money. I had gotten past the rough patch when I stopped thinking about how tired I had become.

This is when your breakthrough is going to come, and this is when my breakthrough came! Encouragement is your fuel needed to move on. It's like being on an escalator moving up to the next level.

Getting Tired Is Part of the Process

Every time you get encouraged, you're being encouraged to do better. You are being encouraged to excel and set your sights on greater things that you never imagined you could do. Now you are bringing your "A" game, where you can experience the thrill of victory, and have renewed strength to become a heavyweight champion in your field! That's Perseverance 70%.

Chapter 8

The Fruit of Your Labor

HAPPY 80%

There is an old saying "that it's always darkest right before the dawn." If you can just hold on past the humps, past the discouragement, past wanting to quit, you will begin to see the light of abundance coming your way, and the blessing of the fruit of your labor.

Now that I had gotten my second wind and had a renewed determination to succeed, I took my game to the next level. I started to see the fruit of my labor. I was starting to earn $600 and $700 on my jobs, all because of the encouragement I received and because I didn't quit.

Have you ever seen the television series called "The Biggest Loser"? The title of this series is really a play on words, because in reality the *biggest losers* are those who give up on trying to better themselves. However, on "The Biggest Loser" reality television show, there are people who are morbidly obese, some weighing in at over 500 pounds. In order to win, the contestants must lose weight. The one who loses the most weight wins a $250,000 cash prize.

Each episode depicts the struggle, the sweat, and the tears of those individuals in their quest to shed those unwanted pounds. During the course of rigorous exercise and weight loss routines, it shows how difficult it is for the contestants to work off their excess pounds. But it also shows how their coaches encourage them along the way and that every pound they lose is a celebration. This goes to show you that encouragement under tough and even adverse circumstances is enough to keep people motivated to achieve their goals.

Good Labor Starts To Show

Once you start to see the fruits of your labor, everyone else will too, and you will love the validation their compliments bring.

You may have started working out to lose weight and wanted to quit, but you received the encouragement you needed to keep going. With that encouragement, you now have revived strength and a renewed desire to lose weight. You may have struggled with the Spanish class you signed up for, but you didn't quit because you received encouragement to keep going. Now, you are much better at speaking Spanish.

If we were to put the compass on where are you in your progress for the "Make it Your Season" challenge, you would see that you are heading in the right direction to be a winner. You would also see that you are at the same point I was, when I went from making $300 a night to making $700 a night. So don't be discouraged. You are doing well!

Letting Nothing Get In Your Way

Now you will not let anything get between you and your routines because you know the importance of not quitting, therefore, you make the time to work out. You have time set aside to study. You make time for any seasonal choice you have. Your seasonal choice is now becoming a part of your life. Whatever you have to do to keep you moving closer to your goal, keep at it. Whatever gets in the way of your goal, get rid of it.

Repetition Rules

Repetition really pays off. Did you know that research has shown that after a person does something for sixty-six consecutive days, it becomes a habit? For example, can you remember when you first started driving a car and you used to look at the gear shift to make sure it was in gear? At first you were not confident enough in your shifting not to look. Do you remember counting the times it took to shift into reverse (one shift)? Counting the times it took to shift into neutral (two shifts)? And counting the shifts, or even looking at the dashboard, to put the car into drive (three shifts)?

Do you remember that you used to be the hesitant driver shifting gears with full concentration? That is, until you started driving every day and became accustomed to the counts on the gear shift. Only after driving a lot did it become second nature, allowing you to do it without looking at the steering column. Just like your drive pattern becomes a habit, the same pattern of habits also translates into all areas of life.

That is why you want to develop good habits for the success you would like to achieve. The fruits of your labor is Happy 80%.

Chapter 9

It's Your Season!

WON THE LOTTERY 90%

If you have been following along with me and have implemented my system for success, the moment you've been waiting for is finally here! You have walked the road to success and have taken the following steps. You found out what you want. You took a step in the right direction. You've gotten into the world of what you want. You've learned the importance of having a mentor. You've started seeing results. You've learned not to quit, because you've just gotten started. You've learned that getting tired is part of the process, and you've started seeing the fruits of your labor. GREAT!

You have reached another milestone, because you have graduated from "habit" to "lifestyle." That's right, your seasonal choice is no longer a habit because habits can be broken. Your seasonal choice is now officially your lifestyle, and the result of your lifestyle is showing. It is evident you are doing well and everyone can see it. You have exercised and lost weight, now people can see your dream body. You have earned that college degree, now people will know that you're educated. You're a better parent, and your children have confirmed it. You have cultivated good habits, developed an effective routine, maintained your discipline, and now you have a successful lifestyle in that area. By sticking with your seasonal choice, you feel like you won the lottery—but it's not over. Why? The answer is simple. Just because you have completed one seasonal choice won't bring you to completion. You have to complete all the lacking areas of your life, in order to make that visual you have of your dream life come true.

Let me give you an example of a life that has completed multiple seasonal choices. Picture that you are having a dinner party for some close friends and getting everything together. Then also imagine preparing a list for everything that you would need to host this wonderful occasion. Then imagine yourself being able to go to any grocery store you want to purchase all the groceries you will need but without any concern about cost.

Then also imagine yourself looking good in your fine clothes that you, the host, are wearing. Then imagine you being there in your immaculately clean and fabulously furnished house, having substantive conversations on hot topics and current events with your guests. And most of all, imagine the love and laughter that you share with your guests, that spills out from your heart that is filled with happiness and joy all because you are complete from fulfilling multiple seasonal choices. Doesn't imagining all of this make you feel great? This is what you can experience by achieving multiple seasonal choices to make that dream life come true.

Choose Discipline

The whole key to mastering any seasonal choice is the discipline it takes to make it a part of your life. Discipline is developing the training and skills needed in order to mold your life to what you want it to be. However, there are no short cuts in discipline because the results will show for themselves.

For example, whenever Chicago Bulls champion Michael Jordan hit the game winning shot, that was the result of discipline. That game winning shot only takes a second of time, but is the result of countless hours spent in a gym being faithful and consistent to practicing and shooting drills.

Discipline means, if you have to get up at 5:00 in the morning to work out, five days a week, then you do exactly that. You don't get up at 7:30, and only workout for two days instead. If you do that, the results will show. Therefore, in order to make it your season, you must have discipline as a part of your life.

"Remember" that not only can you use this system for one part of your life, you can use it on all parts of your life to make this life the one that you want. That is how you make it your season. You make the life that you want one step at a time and you're going to be happy. Nothing is going to stand in the way of you getting what you want, because you have everything you need in order to be successful.

My Season

Let me take a brief detour and share something with you that is absolutely awesome. After making photography my seasonal choice and carefully working my system, I was fortunate enough to land my own setup in a lounge where I was the photographer. I also began taking photos of celebrities. Just as I always believed, I began making thousands of dollars per night. I had been using all the techniques that I learned from all the photographers I had ever met. Now I'm at optimal capacity and the top of my game. The system for success that I developed was working so well for me that it became obvious to everyone that I had arrived because of all the money flowing in.

As a matter of fact, it was so clear to everyone, that the photographer at Couture City Lounge that mentored me was now asking me about my secret for success. That's when I started to share my system with him. Amazingly, it was like a role reversal. The person, from whom I received instruction, was now asking instructions from me on how to improve his skills. Imagine that! Now I had become a giant to him, just as he was the giant to me. And you too, will have this effect on your mentor when you're doing well.

My Other Seasonal Choices

At this point, you might ask, what were my other seasonal choices? Well, in chapter one, I already discussed two seasonal choices, which were establishing a relationship with God and doing a complete makeover of my finances. But there was more to it than that—here are the rest.

My third seasonal choice was to *be-*

come organized. The opposite of being organized is chaos, and wherever there is chaos it's almost impossible to make progress. Being organized means putting everything in order. So I started in my house. I threw away all the clutter that was taking up space. I threw away old papers and magazines. I got rid of old shoes, clothes, and appliances that no longer worked. I got rid of everything that was taking up space that no longer had any purpose or use. Before getting organized, it used to take me twenty minutes just to find the mate to a sock. But today I have solved all those clutter and time-wasting issues by being organized. What I love most about being organized is I can find all my important documents or any object I need with my eyes closed. My clothes and my socks are in their proper places because I'm totally organized.

My fourth seasonal choice was to *become debt-free.* I was tired of all the letters and phone calls from bill collectors. So I took charge of my debt and worked to pay it all off to the tune of $21,000. I obtained a copy of my credit report and contacted each creditor and made arrangements to pay off the debt. I also paid off all my parking tickets. Though it took some doing, I successfully eliminated all of my debt. The part that I love most about being debt-free is I can now spend my money on things like taking trips to Hawaii.

My fifth seasonal choice was to *master eating properly*. Even before I improved my diet, I always wanted to eat right but just couldn't afford the healthier organic foods. However, I started eating right by eliminating unhealthy things like fast food that are usually fried/greasy and loaded with fat, cholesterol, and salt.

I also eliminated sugary items like soda and started eating many more fresh fruits, colorful vegetables, and organic foods. Now I shop at the grocery store a lot more and cook at home. What I love most about eating properly is that I feel great in my body and I have the energy I need to carry out a productive day. By having all the nutrients I need, I don't get fatigued like I used to when I always ate on the go.

My sixth and final seasonal choice was *regular exercise.* I developed a workout routine that worked for me. I don't try to overdo it, or set unrealistic expectations. I exercise three to four times a week. By keeping consistent with exercise and a proper diet, I lost over forty pounds. What I love most about exercising is it has allowed me to drop clothes sizes. I love my attire now. And I was able to get a new wardrobe, and I feel so alive in my clothes. I have the look that I always wanted. Life is good.

Looking back on it, I am so happy that I stuck with all my seasonal choices, because truly I am living the life that I have always desired. I'm in my season and feel like I won the Lottery, 90%.

Chapter 10

Managing Your Season

WATCHFUL 100%

One of the biggest enemies to progress is the failure to keep moving forward. Forward motion takes work. The only time forward motion doesn't require effort is when you are headed downhill—that's not the direction you want to go.

Unfortunately, that's what happens to many people after achieving some level of success, they stop moving forward. After reaching their ideal weight, for whatever reason, they stop working out, stop their routine and ditch their diet. They get complacent. Complacency is the worst enemy of progress, because you get to the point where you feel "I've made it, and this is enough."

> *"You can never be satisfied with 'this is enough' because when that happens, you're automatically headed downhill."*

That's why a day in my life is surrounded by me looking to better manage my six seasonal choices. Here are six ways that I achieve that: (1) Staying sharp on my spirituality by reading inspirational commentaries daily. (2) Making sure my investments are sound by being diligent in research before I invest my hard earned money. (3) Staying relevant on the happenings at the life improvement stores like Ikea/Container stores so I can stay organized. (4) Obtaining a copy of my credit report and keeping track on my credit score two/three times a year, and by monitoring any debt that I may have incurred and need to pay off. (5) Staying on the hunt for new and exciting vegetables I've never experienced, and purchasing new cook books to see the seasonal trends that I would enjoy cooking. (6) Taking some friends to the gym to workout with and subscribing to the health food store's e-mail list and newsletter for details on the benefits of new supplements.

General Management

You have to continue to stay relevant and continue to grow. You must have the foresight to see the new trends coming on a global level, then capitalize on them by updating and adjusting to those new trends.

For example, General Motors (GM) almost folded because they were not making enough fuel-efficient cars like some foreign and other domestic car manufacturers. Car buyers had been spoiled with cars that were getting better miles per gallon.

Before GM went completely under, the government gave them billions of dollars to bail them out. After that, GM started making more fuel-efficient cars to keep up with their competition. If the government wouldn't have bailed out GM, they would have folded because they failed to manage their season by keeping up with auto trends and producing fuel-efficient cars.

Therefore, it is important to stay informed and to keep striving for greater heights. Continue to read trade magazines. Continue to upgrade equipment and keep up to date on techniques in your field. Continue to stay current on industry changes and trends that can affect how or where to do business, or you can become outdated. You must take charge in managing your season.

Managing Photography

For example, I couldn't be satisfied with just making thousands of dollars a night, using back drop photography. Because with the invention of cell phone cameras, I started to lose money. People were bypassing me and would simply take photos with their cell phone camera and then upload them to Facebook. So in response to this change in the industry, I stayed relevant in photography by taking a class in Photoshop, which is a computer program that professionals use. There are many things you can do with Photoshop that you can't do with any other program or cell phone. I can perform tricks like changing the backgrounds on photos and even removing tattoos people don't want shown in their photos. I can even add graphics and people's names to photos. My income had started to decline because of the cell phone camera technology boom, but now by using Photoshop to manage my season, I'm still on top.

    I also developed a website, and I always purchase new backdrops and more photography equipment. Online, I also utilize social media like Facebook. With my Facebook page I can keep an active friends list, stay in contact with all my friends, and keep them updated on events and specials that my company is offering. All of this growth and advancement is a great marketing tool for staying in demand. When people see me managing my seasonal choice, it encourages them to want to utilize my services even more. As I stay in touch with friends and potential customers, they can't wait to see what's new. Once again, managing your season is the only way to stay effective and on top of your game.

Farewell Season

Finally, just as seasons are subject to change, so do seasonal choices. With me being successful personally and professionally, my seasonal choices are changing. By me using this system for at least six areas of my life and seeing it work, I've come to the realization that this system can work on anything. Therefore, my latest seasonal choices are the biggest one's ever. The dream that I have now is an early retirement from barbering and photography to transition into being the world's greatest motivational speaker and live my passion of helping people full-time by becoming a "Make it Your Season" life coach, because I love to motivate and inspire people more than anything in the world.

The main point that I want to stress in this book is that make it your season is about you getting to the point where you are past the simple parts of life.

"This book was written so you can soar upon the wings of your passion, and challenge all your obstacles to accomplish your biggest dreams."

It is essential to choose some seasonal choices and make them a part of your life. Then pick some more choices and make them a part of your lifestyle. Keep using this system until you get to the choices that you are most passionate about. That's how you get to your "dream life" and discover the Mega-million feeling without playing the lottery.

Ever since I was a kid, I was always a big dreamer. People used to laugh at me and think I was talking nonsense because I never wanted/settled for the status quo. I always pushed for more than what was being offered. For example, if the average person makes $1000 a week from working, I wanted to make that amount in one day and "I did."

My motto is: "You only get one chance at life, so do well and dream Big."

After challenging myself on many levels in life and succeeding, my confidence has increased even more. Just as my confidence has increased, my goals have increased too. So even with my career changes on the horizon, I want to add the cherry to the sundae of thinking Big. I'm looking for "Ten Million" people to Make It Their Season, and to help with this endeavor I have launched a real cool website where I will be helping people get solutions in life.

The website is a social networking site with a Purpose. The website is set up so that when you create an account you can choose a seasonal choice and track your percentages online. You also can blog about the progress you are making toward making it your season, while waiting on opportunity to increase the percentage level you have achieved. You can also upload photos that you would like to share and see how the other members are doing with their percentages. Best of all, it's free of charge. Please go to www.MakeItYourSeason.com for more details and to take the Make It Your Season challenge. Thank you for allowing me to share my proven strategy for Success with you, and I encourage you to join me in *Making This Your Season*. Watchful 100%.☺

www.ingramcontent.com/pod-product-compliance
Lightning Source LLC
Chambersburg PA
CBHW031200160426
43193CB00008B/450